KU-356-541

Creative PHOTOGRAPHY

Russ Malkin

Kingfisher Books

For Mum, Dad and Chris

Kingfisher Books, Grisewood and Dempsey Ltd,
Elsley House, 24–30 Great Titchfield Street,
London W1P 7AD

First published in paperback in 1993 by Kingfisher Books
2 4 6 8 10 9 7 5 3
Originally published in hardback in 1990 by Kingfisher Books

Text and illustrations © Grisewood & Dempsey Ltd 1990
Photographs © Russ Malkin 1990

All rights reserved. No part of this publication may
be reproduced, stored in a retrieval system or
transmitted by any means, electronic, mechanical,
photocopying or otherwise, without the prior permission
of the publisher.

BRITISH LIBRARY CATALOGUING IN PUBLICATION DATA
A catalogue record for this book is available
from the British Library

ISBN 0 86272 920 3

Edited by Annabel Warburg and Nicola Barber
Designed by Robert Wheeler
Photographs by Russ Malkin
Illustrations by Kuo Kang Chen
Cover design by Terry Woodley
Camera on front cover courtesy of Konica UK Ltd
Phototypeset by Wyvern Typesetting, Bristol, England
Printed in Spain

CONTENTS

PANORAMA

Have you ever wanted to capture on film a beautiful landscape or a long beach or a view over a city, only to find that you cannot squeeze it all into one picture? By taking a series of photographs one next to another you can build up a panoramic photograph of the whole scene. Panoramas are easy to do; the results are guaranteed to impress.

HOW TO TAKE YOUR PANORAMA

1. Find a spot where you can see the whole view that you want to photograph. It is important when taking the series of photographs that you do not move from this spot.

2. Start from the farthest point on the left and take the first photograph.

3. Try and keep the camera level and the horizon at the same height in the viewfinder as you move the camera to the right.

SAFETY FILM

Top Tip
Try holding the camera vertically . . . the results can be even more impressive!

► 33A   ► 34

The single photograph above cannot capture the whole scene, but the panorama below does.

Keep the camera level as you take your photographs.

SAFETY FILM

Top Tip
Avoid having objects in the foreground.

▶ 33A
▶ 34 ∘

4. Make sure that you have about a third of your first picture in the viewfinder before you take the second photograph. This overlap ensures that you do not miss any of the view and helps you to join the photographs together later.

5. Keep taking photographs, each one overlapping the previous one, until the whole scene has been covered.

Note the overlap of the photographs.

HOW TO MAKE YOUR PANORAMA

You will need:
scissors
a ruler
sticky tape – preferably masking tape or any tape that can be peeled off the photograph without spoiling it
a sharp pencil

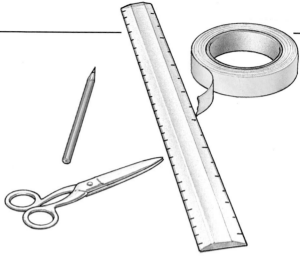

1. Lay all your photographs on the floor to get an impression of how your panorama will look. You may notice that you cannot match up each photograph exactly to its neighbour and that there is a slight curve to the panorama. Do not worry about this.

The eye line in this photograph is the edge of the water.

2. Pick a line that runs across the panorama: it could be the horizon, the sea's edge on the beach, a fence or a row of houses. When joining the photographs together this line must match up from one photograph to the next. We shall call this the **'eye line'**.

3. Start on the left and lay the first photograph down. Lay the next one down so that they overlap, and match up the eye line. Keep both photographs parallel and then carefully stick them together at top and bottom with tape that can be pulled off easily.

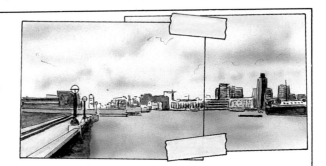

4. Pick a point half way along the overlap of the two photographs and, using the ruler and pencil, draw a vertical line down the top photograph. Cut along this line with the scissors and remove the tape.

5. Join the two photographs together again, making sure the eye line matches. Using a small piece of tape, stick the two photographs together. Turn them both over and stick them together securely. Remove the tape on the front.

Make sure the sticky tape peels off easily.

6. Repeat this process for all the photographs and gradually build up your panorama.

SAFETY FILM

Top Tip
Stick your panorama on some card and hang it on the wall.

► 33A ► 34

7. The top of the photographs may not all line up but when the panorama is finished, cut along the top and bottom so that they are level.

Trim the panorama along top and bottom.

MONTAGE

This is a similar idea to the panorama, but rather than recording a scene as one strip of photographs, a montage is like a jigsaw of pictures. A montage is a fun and effective way of photographing large scenes and interiors.

HOW TO TAKE YOUR MONTAGE

As in the panorama, you take a series of photographs, each of which overlaps its neighbour. It is important to take the photographs in a systematic order to avoid missing any of the scene.

1. Stand near the edge of the scene or in the corner of the room you want to photograph and stay in the same spot while taking the photographs.

2. Starting at the top left, take your first photograph and work across the scene to the right, making sure each photograph overlaps its neighbour. Work across a second row, making sure that there is some overlap at the top with the photographs of the first row. Repeat the process until you have covered the whole scene.

3. If you are not sure whether you have covered the scene, take a few more photographs, otherwise there may be a large gap in the final montage.

SAFETY FILM

Top Tip
For fun include your pets twice in the montage.

▶ 33A   ▶ 34

SAFETY FILM

Top Tip
To begin with, practise by taking four photos for your first montage.

▶ 33A   ▶ 34

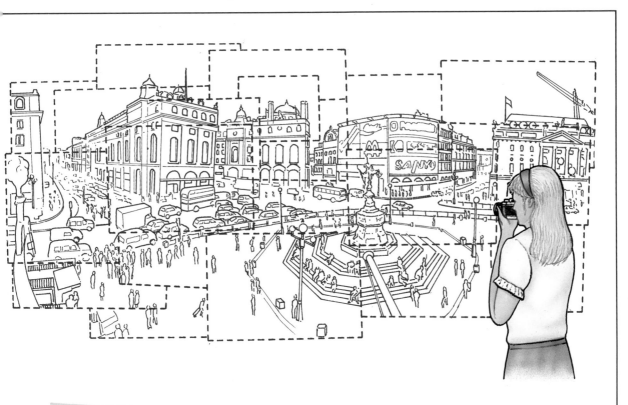

Piccadilly Circus, London

HOW TO MAKE YOUR MONTAGE

You will need:
sticky tape (preferably masking tape—
make sure the tape can be peeled off
the photos easily)
scissors (be very careful when cutting the
photographs)
a ruler

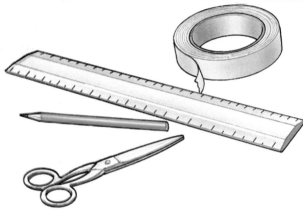

1. Lay all the photographs on tne floor
to get an idea of how your montage will
look.

You won't be able to match
everything up perfectly and you
may notice that the montage tends
to curve round.

2. Experiment to find which is the best
way to overlap the photographs. Pick
the most effective arrangement.
Starting at the top left, pick out the first
two photographs without disturbing the
rest of the arrangement.

3. Overlap the two photographs and line
them up as best you can. Tape them
together. Mark a line half way along the
overlap and cut along this line through
both photographs. Remove the tape.

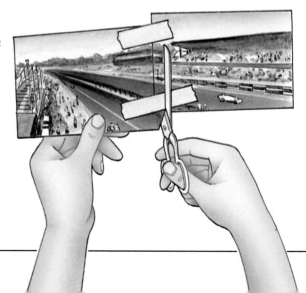

4. Join the two photographs together again with a small piece of tape on the front. Turn the photographs over and stick them securely together down the back.

5. Repeat this for all the photographs. Sometimes you may have to cut out extra corners for the best effect, but take your time and ask for advice from a friend or an adult if you need it.

6. Be sure that all the photographs are stuck together on the back before removing the tape from the front. Leave the edges of the final montage uneven – it looks more effective.

You can now stick your montage onto a sheet of card and hang it on the wall for everyone to admire.

PICTURE PUZZLES

Have fun photographing everyday objects at close range and from unusual angles. See if your friends can recognize what the mystery object is before you show them the picture that reveals the secret!

If you want to photograph an object at close range, be sure you can keep it in focus. As a rule do not get any closer than one metre. Pick objects that are quite large and remember to photograph them from an unusual angle.

POP GROUP QUIZ

Think of some pop groups whose names can be suggested by photographs:
For example, the groups suggested by these photographs are 'Queen', and 'The Four Tops'.

Top Tip
Avoid small detail in the picture that will give it away.

Top Tip
Display the photos upside down to make identification even more difficult!

Display your puzzles by sticking them in a book with the close-up photographs at the front and the answers at the back.

CRAZY CAPTIONS

Take an amusing photograph and write a funny caption underneath.
Hang the photograph on the wall and ask others to think of an amusing caption as well.

I'm working on a lead and I think you might be able to help.

What's up, Doc?

Top Tip
Try and have someone's mouth open so that it looks as though they are speaking.

13

MAKE YOUR OWN CARDS

These are cheaper than buying cards from a shop and they are fun to make and to receive.
The card can be for any special occasion – Christmas, a birthday, a congratulations card, or a get well soon card. The photograph can be of anything you choose.

1. You will need a large sheet of card. You can buy thick, coloured card from an art shop, or a stationer's. It needs to be thick enough to stand up when folded in half. Card that is white on one side will make your message easier to read.

HAPPY CHRISTMAS

HAPPY BIRTHDAY

GOOD LUCK

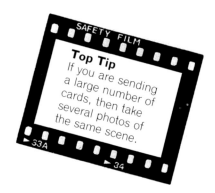

Top Tip
If you are sending a large number of cards, then take several photos of the same scene.

14

3. Mark out with a ruler the size of card you need. Remember that it has to fold in two.

4. Cut the card out and fold it in two. Place your photograph on the front.

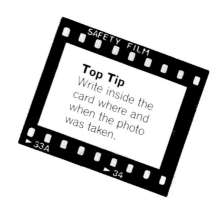

Top Tip
Write inside the card where and when the photo was taken.

2. Choose the photograph that you are going to send and lay it on your card. Leave at least a two-centimetre border around all sides and leave a wider border at the bottom.

5. Glue your photograph down and press, making sure that all the corners are firmly in place. You can decorate the border with felt pen, glue and glitter or coloured stickers. Write your message beneath the picture and inside the card.

PHOTO DIARY

Instead of, or as well as, writing a diary every day or week, start a Photo Diary. It could contain pictures of places you have visited, people you have met, and activities you have taken part in.

You don't have to have a photograph for every day. Perhaps once a week take a photograph of somewhere you have been, or friends at school. Find a large book with plain or lined pages and use this as your Photo Diary.

15th July

This morning I played football with some friends in the square.

As a special treat, our swimming class went snorkelling at the beach in the afternoon.

Stick each photograph in the book and write underneath all the information about the picture that you can think of.

Remember to date the page.

Top Tip
Photograph your friends. You may see them every day now, but that may not always be so.

Top Tip
Make sure the book you buy has at least 52 pages, for one photograph a week.

26th September

We went riding in the country.

The view was fantastic. We met some cows on the way.

Stick the photographs into the book with glue that doesn't make the writing on the other side of the page run or smudge. Double-sided sticky tape works well. You could also stick things like tickets, labels and postcards in your diary, or add your own drawings.

A DAY IN THE LIFE OF . . .

It could be a day in the life of you, a friend, or your whole family. It could be a day's outing or just a normal day at school . . .

The idea is to have about eight photographs that tell the story of what happened during one day. You then stick the photographs on a large piece of card or in a book and write captions under each photograph explaining what is happening.

Begin with a photograph at the start of the day, waking up, eating breakfast or getting dressed. Make sure that all the following photographs capture the main scenes of the day.

A DAY OUT WITH MY BROTHER

1 *I had to get up early, but I had time to eat breakfast before leaving to catch the train.*

2
We went to a museum. The queue was too long, so we headed for the park.

3
Some of the swans were nearly as big as me!

4
Here's my friend Bill!

HOW TO DISPLAY YOUR PHOTOGRAPHS

1. From all of the photographs that you have taken, select the eight that best represent the whole day from start to finish.

2. Find a piece of thick card that is large enough to take all of the photographs.

3. Lay the photographs onto the card, making sure there is room for all the captions. Then stick the photographs down.

4. Write your captions and put the title in big letters at the top.

SAFETY FILM

Top Tip
Take some funny photographs so that you can write an amusing caption later.

SAFETY FILM

Top Tip
Don't be afraid to set up a shot, or recreate a good picture that you missed.

6

The geese were so tame. I was feeding this one bread straight from my hand.

5 *Andy decided he wanted a hamburger for lunch. I had a hot dog.*

7 *This squirrel must have had lunch. He wasn't interested in Andy's peanuts.*

8 *Great! A cup of tea after a busy day.*

STORY BOARD

A story board is similar to a comic but instead of using cartoon characters, the figures are real people. Get together with some friends and write a story that can be told in 10 or 12 pictures.

1. Decide who is going to take the photographs and who is going to act. Someone can be the Director and it is their job to make sure everyone is in the right place and that the location is suitable.

2. The aim is to make each photograph tell a story. The Director should position the actors correctly and make sure that those people who are supposed to be speaking have their mouths open.

Top Tip
Check the list of Common Mistakes (page 26–29) before you begin.

3. Take the film to the developer's. When all the photographs are developed, choose the ones that you need and stick them on to a large piece of card.

4. Now comes the fun part – using 'speech bubbles'.
On a piece of white paper or card draw speech bubbles of various sizes to fit each photograph. Write in the words that person is supposed to be saying. Cut out the speech bubbles and stick them on to the photographs, matching them up with the right people. You can also add captions under the photographs to explain what is happening.

Top Tip
Take a couple of pictures for each scene, varying the angle slightly.

After a game of tennis Steven, Rob, Liz and Sasha have nothing to do.

Steven has an idea.

The friends decide who will act and who will organize.

The story has to be written down first. They decide that the story will be about a tennis match.

Shooting starts.

The girls play their game as Steven plans the pictures for the story board and Rob takes the photographs.

The game finishes and the last photo is taken. The film is taken to be processed.

The friends go through their photographs to select the ones to use on the story

TIME LAPSE

A photograph is one of the best ways of recording the passage of time. Here are some ways of using photographs to show how times change.

OLD AND NEW

Go through all your very old photographs or, even better, go to the library to see if you can get some old pictures of your neighbourhood, perhaps as postcards or in old newspapers. Pick the oldest one you can find of a place that you know. Then go there and take a photograph from exactly the same spot as the old photograph.

Try this with a number of different places and put the pictures in a book. It is fascinating to see how places, people and fashions change.

A picture of a High Street in 1901.

The same view in 1990.

YOU

Collect a picture of yourself every year. Stick them in a book with the date. When you are older, you will be amazed to see how much you have changed.

7th October 1979. Aged 8.

8th June 1972 Aged 18 months.

2nd May 1992 Aged 21.

Rainy autumn afternoon.

Sunny summer's morning.

THE SEASONS AND WEATHER

Choose a view that you see regularly and take a photograph of it every time the seasons change and in different weathers. As you collect the photographs, stick them in a book noting when they were taken. When you have a whole year of photographs, you'll be surprised to see how much the same scene can change.

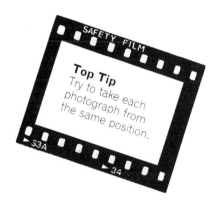

Top Tip
Try to take each photograph from the same position.

And here is high tide.

If you do not want to wait long for a change in your scene, find something that changes quite quickly. For instance here we have a low tide.

Top Tip
Ask someone to remind you . . . it's easy to forget to take the photographs.

23

FAMILY TREE

It is fun searching through old photographs. By putting them together as a family tree, it provides you and your family with a photographic record of your history.

1. The object is to find a photograph of every member of your family as far back as you can go. Start with your grandparents. You may choose just to explore one side of your family first. Find photographs of your grandparents, your aunts and uncles and their children (your cousins). As you collect the photos, find out when and where each person was born. The more information the better – but remember it all has to fit on to a chart.

SAFETY FILM

Top Tip
Keep all the photographs about the same size: about 5cm by 7½cm.

► 33A   ► 34

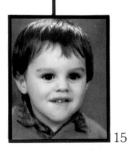

1. William Dennett.
2. Molly Dennett. Married 1931.
3. Anthony V. Malkin. Sales Manager.
4. Jill Malkin. Married 1954.
5. Shirley Ann Taylor. Married 1956.
6. Kenneth Taylor. Baker. European Sailing Champion.
7. Lucy Malkin. Married 1978.
8. Gary V. Malkin. Born 1957. Salesman.
9. Steven M. Malkin. Racing Driver.

24

2. Some of the photographs will be too big to stick on to a chart and some will be too valuable to cut up, so you will have to copy them using your camera.

3. Lay the photograph on a flat surface, making sure it is flat. Stick the corners down with pins or some masking tape (this tape will pull off the photograph without tearing or marking it).

4. Get as close to the photograph as your camera will allow and make sure the picture is in focus. Be sure that you have enough light and that there are no reflections coming off the picture. Try photographing using sunlight.

5. When you have assembled all of your photographs, place them on a large sheet of paper and arrange them in order. Draw lines to show the children of each set of parents. When you are happy that it all makes sense (check with your family) stick the photographs down.

Top Tip
Take your photograph from directly above the one you are copying.

SAFETY FILM
►33A ►34

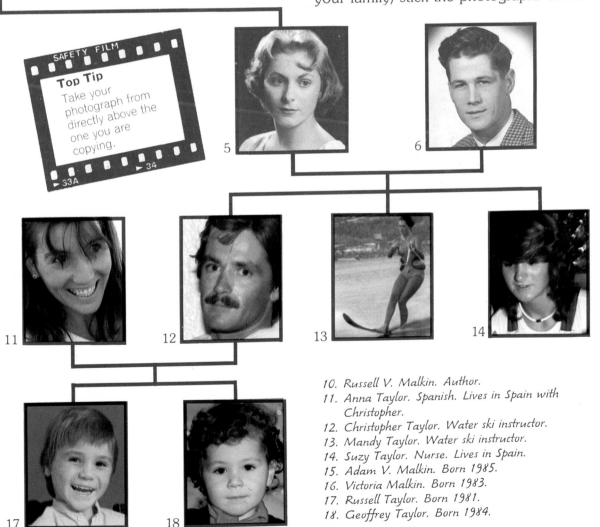

10. Russell V. Malkin. Author.
11. Anna Taylor. Spanish. Lives in Spain with Christopher.
12. Christopher Taylor. Water ski instructor.
13. Mandy Taylor. Water ski instructor.
14. Suzy Taylor. Nurse. Lives in Spain.
15. Adam V. Malkin. Born 1985.
16. Victoria Malkin. Born 1983.
17. Russell Taylor. Born 1981.
18. Geoffrey Taylor. Born 1984.

COMMON MISTAKES

Have you ever taken photographs that are out of focus, blurred, over exposed or badly composed? Here is some advice on how to avoid making common mistakes that spoil photographs.

1. FINGER IN THE SHOT

Make sure your fingers are well away from the camera lens and also from any exposure meters that are on the front of the camera. Remember that on some cameras the lens that you look through is not the same lens that takes the photograph.

2. OUT OF FOCUS

Although there are many cameras, there are only four types of focusing system:
a) It can be pre-set by the manufacturer – so you cannot change the focus. Make sure the subject is at least one metre from you and take the picture in as much light as possible.
b) There may be a choice of symbols that you have to select (*see below*). Try and adjust your composition to match one symbol.
c) You focus the camera yourself by adjusting the lens. If photographing people, always focus on the eyes.
d) Autofocus. Keep the main object you are photographing in the centre of the picture.

Head and shoulders – approximately 1 metre away.

Full body – approximately 2–3 metres away.

Landscape – anything over 3 metres.

3. BLURRED

Sometimes this can be mistaken for a photograph that is out of focus. Blurred photographs are caused by the camera or the subject moving during exposure. To avoid it, try and take your photographs in as much light as possible. If you are photographing a moving subject, move the camera with the action (See *Sports Assignment on page 34*). Hold the camera still and, if necessary, use a chair or a wall to steady the camera. Make sure that you are standing properly.

Top Tip
Practise holding your camera in front of a mirror to check where your fingers lie.

Use a wall or a chair to help steady your camera in low light conditions.

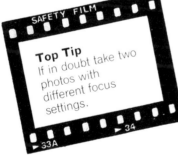

Top Tip
If in doubt take two photos with different focus settings.

4. RED EYE

Flash photos can make people's eyes look red. To avoid this, keep your back to a bright light so when your subjects look towards the camera their eyes will react to the light behind you. Their pupils will become much smaller and this will reduce the 'red eye' effect. Some cameras have an 'anti-red-eye' feature that sends out bright light just before the flash goes off.

27

5. FLARE

If you take a photograph with the camera pointing towards the sun, the light may reflect off the lens and make strange patterns on your photograph. You may not even see this through the viewfinder. To avoid flare, do not point the camera towards the sun.

▲ Never point your camera into the sun.

Top Tip
The sun should be behind you when taking a photograph.

◀ Colour distortion and dots can occur in your photographs.

6. OVER-/UNDER-EXPOSURE

Sometimes if there is a variation in the amount of light in different parts of your picture, the camera's exposure system can be fooled. This means that your prints can be too light or too dark. Try and take photographs of scenes where the light is evenly distributed. Be careful when taking photographs in the snow as the camera will take a reading off the snow and will not expose your subject properly.

▼ Under-exposed – the photo is too dark.

▶ Over-exposed – the photo is too pale.

7. POOR COMPOSITION

Remember to check the whole picture before taking a shot, particularly the background. The classic mistake is to have a tree behind the subject. It may make them look like a triffid! (*See Landscape Assignment on page 30*).

Much better: The balloon fills the frame and there is nothing else in the shot to distract.

Poor composition: the foreground is too cluttered and the balloon is not very prominent.

8. FOGGED OR BLACK PHOTOS

Errors are often made when the film is either loaded into, or taken out of the camera. When you load the film make sure the film is winding on properly and that the camera back is firmly shut. When taking the film out remember to wind the film back into the cassette completely. If your camera has a motor rewind, wait until this has completely stopped before removing the film. Never open the back of a camera when the film is loaded.

SAFETY FILM

Top Tip
Spend a few seconds checking the scene in your viewfinder before you take the shot.

33A ► 34

Watch out for trees, or in this case balloons, sticking out of people's heads.

29

ASSIGNMENT: LANDSCAPES

Landscapes can be photographs of a beach, a country scene or a view over your town or village. They are a general view of a large area, and because of this it is sometimes difficult to make them interesting.

Here are a few tips that can help:

● BREAK THE PHOTOGRAPH DOWN INTO THREE parts. Have something occurring in the foreground, the middle and the background. This gives the photograph depth and helps to lead the eye into the picture.

SAFETY FILM

Top Tip
Make sure the closest object is at least three metres away.

33A   34

Here the scene is broken down into foreground (the boys), middleground (the bridge), and background (the person through the arch). This will give the photograph depth.

● TRY AND FRAME THE FOREGROUND WITH a tree, a fence or a building.

● TAKE PLENTY OF TIME LOOKING FOR THE best shot. Get as high as possible and start by looking at the scene with the branches of a tree hanging across one corner of the photograph.

In this case the trees work well as a frame for the scene.

● IMAGINE BREAKING YOUR PHOTOGRAPH INTO three roughly equal vertical sections. Try and make any major feature in the picture occur at these third points. For example a church, or a tree, or a boat. Avoid having the main points of interest right in the middle of the frame. Do the same horizontally as well. Have the horizon one third down from the top.

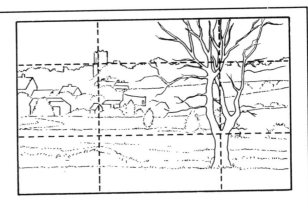

Avoid having any major features right in the middle of the picture. Break the scene down into thirds horizontally and vertically and have features occur at these points. This helps to balance the photograph.

● LOOK FOR WALLS, FENCES, HEDGES or roads that lead your eye into the picture. Don't take the first photograph that presents itself. Look around for a few seconds and try and improve it.

▲ Always look for colour. Bright colours and different shapes make a photograph stand out.

◄ Look for lines that draw the eye into the photograph. It can be a fence, a wall, or in this case, a beach.

ASSIGNMENT: PEOPLE AND ANIMALS

The problem with photographing people and animals is that they keep moving! This can be an advantage, as you can direct them into the position that you want.

PEOPLE

● Setting up a photograph need not take long – the quicker you do it the better, as some people may get distracted.

Sometimes people can find it difficult to relax in front of a camera, so try taking pictures without them knowing.

Photograph people in their everyday surroundings.

Top Tip
Do not have too much sky above the head.

Top Tip
Get the people in your photograph to smile.

Hold the camera vertically to fill the frame.

● When taking a photograph of one person or sometimes even two people, try holding the camera vertically. This avoids having empty spaces down the sides of the photo. Also when photographing one person avoid getting the whole body in. Move in a little closer to make the photograph less formal.

● If you do want to set up a group photograph, make sure everyone is relaxed and that the picture is not too formal. They do not all have to be standing shoulder to shoulder. Have some of the group sitting and frame the photograph with the tallest people at the sides.

● Always focus on the eyes. In a group shot, focus on a person who is in the middle, not the person closest to you.

Always carry a camera; you never know who you might meet!

ANIMALS

Now for the hard one . . . Try and capture the fun side of your pet or the animal that you are photographing.

● As with people, some of the best pictures are taken when the subjects are unaware that they are being photographed. You will need patience and a quick eye to wait for a good picture to present itself and to capture it on film.

You can always use food to attract the attention of animals. The dogs in this photograph were looking at some biscuits held by someone on my right.

Top Tip
When photographing animals, always take some of their favourite food.

The ducks (left) were being fed bread and the squirrel (right) was eating a peanut.

● Get to know the subject that you are photographing. If you can anticipate what the animal is going to do, you stand a better chance of capturing the picture. Your photograph will be much more interesting if the animal is doing something.

● Find the best angle. It may be better to get as low to the ground as possible. Animals photographed from above do not look so good. Also avoid having confusing backgrounds.

33

ASSIGNMENT: SPORTS

The secret here is: be prepared. In most sports you can predict where most of the action is going to take place, for example in the goal mouth at a football match, at home base in softball, at a fence in show jumping. So position yourself as near to one of these points as possible.

● Always follow the action with your camera. Move the camera smoothly and, whenever you want to take a picture, press the shutter gently to avoid jogging the camera.

SAFETY FILM

Top Tip
Try and fill the frame. Don't have a little speck in the middle.

▶ 33A   ▶ 34

This photograph of the baseball game is not very dramatic. The background is too busy and the main area of action is too small.

● If you have the facility on your camera, set it at a high shutter speed, 125th or higher. If you cannot do this, take your photographs with as much light on the subject as possible, move to a sunnier spot or wait for the clouds to disappear.

The serve . . . a good time to predict some action.

Move in closer and wait for the ball. This photograph is much more dynamic.

● Look for the point of action, for example the serve in tennis as the player is concentrating on the ball.

● Keep the background as clear as possible. This will help the subject stand out.

● Take several photographs; do not just rely on one because many of them may be out of focus.

● If you cannot get close to the action, include the crowd and make it a picture that captures the atmosphere of the event, with people cheering or the colours of the different supporters.

The car is kept sharp by moving the camera with the action. The background is uncluttered and lets the car stand out.

Top Tip
Try different angles to make the photo more creative.

SAFETY FILM

Look for colour and fill the frame, even if it means standing in the water!

Try and capture some of the atmosphere of sporting events. The crowd, pictures of preparation or, in this case, the winners on the rostrum.

CAMERAS

All cameras work on the same principle but they can operate in different ways.
There are four basic types of camera.
NOTE: *All the ideas for activities that are explained in this book can be attempted by any of the cameras mentioned below.*

110 viewfinder

35mm compact

autofocus

Typical focus symbols on viewfinder cameras (see page 26).

1. 110 and 126 VIEWFINDER CAMERAS

These cameras take good quality photographs and there are usually three different focus settings. The lens that you look through is not the one that takes the photograph. Also there is no control over which lens, shutter speed or aperture setting to use.

2. 35mm COMPACT AND AUTOFOCUS CAMERAS

The film quality of 35mm is very high. There is some control over the exposure (if required), although most cameras are fully automated. The autofocus cameras will focus for you and many will even wind on and rewind the film for you.

35mm single lens reflex

3. 35mm SINGLE LENS REFLEX CAMERAS

The advantage of these cameras is that you look through the lens that takes the photograph and you can change the lens to one that suits the subject. You also have full control over the exposure of the picture. These cameras are expensive.

4. THE DISPOSABLE CAMERA

This is the most recent camera development. You buy a camera that already has the film sealed inside. The camera is cheap and can only be used once. The whole camera is sent off to the processors and the photographs are then returned to you but not the camera. The focus and exposure are pre-set.

Disposable camera

Fun Disposable Cameras

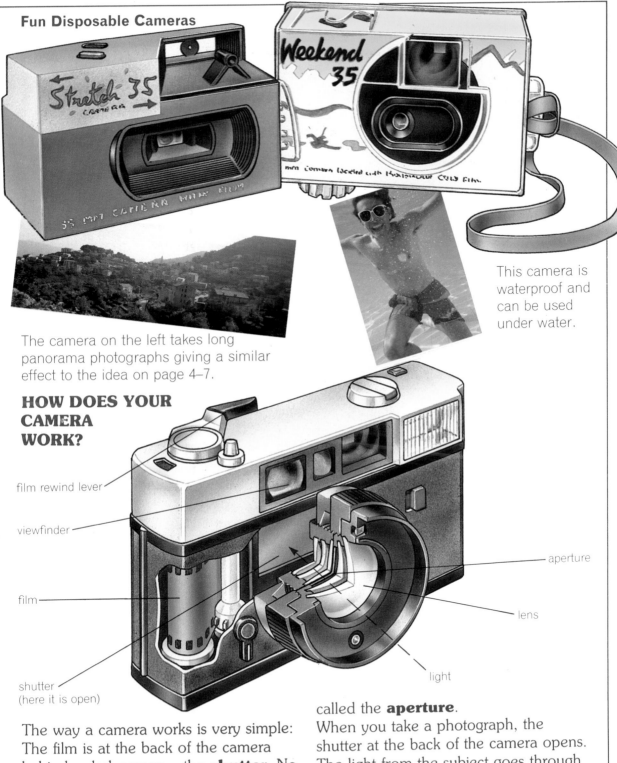

The camera on the left takes long panorama photographs giving a similar effect to the idea on page 4–7.

This camera is waterproof and can be used under water.

HOW DOES YOUR CAMERA WORK?

film rewind lever

viewfinder

film

shutter
(here it is open)

aperture

lens

light

The way a camera works is very simple: The film is at the back of the camera behind a dark screen – the **shutter**. No light can get onto the film until the shutter is open. In front of the shutter is the **lens**. Inside the lens is a hole that can vary in size from the size of a pinhead to the size of a small coin. This is called the **aperture**.

When you take a photograph, the shutter at the back of the camera opens. The light from the subject goes through the lens, aperture and open shutter and onto the film where the photograph is recorded. The shutter then closes, you wind the film on and the camera is ready for the next photograph.

37

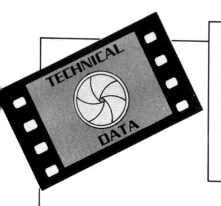

FILM

Although there are many different types of film available, they all fall into two categories – they are either print film or slide film. Unless you intend to use a slide projector to show your photographs, always ask for print film. When buying film you should also specify the type of film, the number of exposures and the film speed.

126mm film

35mm film

110mm film

Always take care when loading your film, and always check that it is winding on between shots.

1. The type of film suitable for your camera. 110, 126 or 35mm (see page 36 to find out the difference).

2. How many exposures you want. This is the number of photographs that can be taken on the film. Normally the choice is 12, 24, or 36 exposures.

3. The speed of the film. Different films react to light in different ways. Choose from the three most common types: 100 ASA, 200 ASA or 400 ASA (ASA is simply a term used to specify film speed). 200 ASA is a good general choice. However, if you expect the light conditions to be dull, use 400 ASA. In bright light use 100 ASA as this gives slightly better quality.

FILM TYPES

1. COLOUR PRINT
Used for most general photography. Can be processed easily and cheaply.

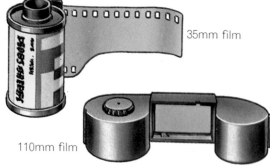

2. SLIDE FILM
Generally more expensive to process than print film and can only be viewed with a slide projector or viewer.

3. BLACK AND WHITE
Black and white is fun to use and can produce very creative and artistic photographs. It is expensive to process and to print.

35mm film
100 ASA
36 exposures

Most films are designed to be used in daylight or with a flash. If you take photographs indoors without a flash you may find the photos have an orange tint. This is because the lights in your house have a warmer glow than sunlight. This effect can spoil the colours in your photographs, so if possible use a flash when photographing indoors.

Indoor shot without a flash

QUALITY OF DAYLIGHT

DAWN Light is clean and there can be a carpet of mist which looks great. No shadows and a slight blue tint.

Dawn

MIDDAY Not a good time to take pictures. The harsh light can cause hard shadows and it can be very hazy.

Midday

SUNSET A good time for a landscape picture. This is the only time when it is advisable to get the sun in your photograph. Watch out for the exposure as the camera can be fooled by areas of dark and light. Take a few photographs varying the amount of sky in each.

Sunset

39

INDEX

KU-356-596

First published 2000 in *The Macmillan Treasury of Nursery Stories*
This collection first published 2010 by Macmillan Children's Books
a division of Macmillan Publishers Limited
20 New Wharf Road, London N1 9RR
Basingstoke and Oxford
Associated companies throughout the world
www.panmacmillan.com

ISBN: 978-0-230-74991-7

This collection copyright © Macmillan Publishers Limited 2010
Text copyright © Mary Hoffman 2000 and 2010
Illustrations copyright © Anna Currey 2000 and 2010
Moral rights asserted.

Every effort has been made to trace the owners of any copyright material in this book but
if any have been inadvertently overlooked the publishers will be pleased to make the
necessary arrangements.

All rights reserved. No part of this publication may be reproduced, stored in or introduced
into a retrieval system, or transmitted in any form, or by any means (electronic,
mechanical, photocopying, recording or otherwise) without the prior written permission
of the publisher. Any person who does any unauthorised act in relation to this publication
may be liable to criminal prosecution and civil claims for damages.

1 3 5 7 9 8 6 4 2

A CIP catalogue record for this book is available from the British Library.

Printed in China

MACMILLAN CHILDREN'S BOOKS

The Three Little Pigs
and other stories

Retold by
Mary Hoffman

Illustrated by
Anna Currey

The Three Little Pigs

There was once an old mother pig who had three piglets. Food was short in their home so, as soon as the three little pigs were old enough, they packed some lunch into their red spotted handkerchiefs and set off to seek their fortune.

The three pigs walked down the road together and met a man carrying a load of straw.

"This is my chance," said the first little pig. "Please give me that straw and I shall build myself a house."

The man gave the pig his straw and the pig built

himself a cosy little house of straw, while his brothers went on their way, still seeking their fortune.

No sooner had the first pig settled himself snugly in his straw house than along came the big bad wolf. He peered through the tiny gap in the straw that the pig had left for a window and saw the chance of a nice dinner for himself.

"Little pig, little pig, let me come in," said the wolf.

"No, no, not by the hairs on my chinny-chin-chin," squeaked the terrified pig. "I'll not let you in."

"Then I'll huff and I'll puff and I'll BLOW YOUR HOUSE DOWN!" said the wolf, and he was as good as his word.

He huffed and he puffed and he blew the straw house right down and gobbled the little pig all up.

As the two other little pigs walked along the road, they met a man carrying a large bundle of twigs.

"Aha," said the second little pig. "This is where I get my chance. Please give me those twigs and I shall build myself a house."

And the man gave him the twigs, while the third little pig carried on seeking his fortune.

The second pig built a house of twigs, which were much stronger than straw. But as soon as he was inside it, there was the eye of the big bad wolf peeping through a space between two twigs and spying on him.

"Little pig, little pig, let me come in," he said.

"No, no, not by the hairs on my chinny-chin-chin," squealed the pig. "I'll not let you in."

"Then I'll huff and I'll puff and I'll BLOW YOUR HOUSE DOWN!" said the wolf, and he was as good as his word.

He huffed and he puffed and he blew the twig house right down and gobbled the little pig all up.

The third pig walked cheerfully along the road, all by himself, until he met a man pushing a barrow full of bricks.

"Please will you give me those bricks, so that I can build a house for myself?" asked the little pig, and the man handed them over.

The pig built himself a really strong house out of bricks, with proper windows and a door and even a chimney. He sat down by his fire and then saw something outside his window. It was the big bad wolf.

"Little pig, little pig, let me come in," said the wolf.

"No, no, not by the hairs on my chinny-chin-chin," said the pig calmly. "I'll not let you in."

"Then I'll huff and I'll puff and I'll BLOW YOUR HOUSE DOWN!" said the wolf.

So the wolf huffed and he puffed. And he puffed and he huffed.

But he could not blow the brick house down.

The wolf was exhausted. And he was also furious. He was determined to eat that little pig.

So the next day he came back and said, "Little pig, I know where there is a good field of turnips."

"Where?" asked the pig.

"In Farmer Smith's field," said the wolf. "I'll take you there at six o'clock tomorrow morning."

The pig agreed but next morning he got up at five o'clock and went to Farmer Smith's field and fetched himself a nice load of turnips and was back in his house before the wolf arrived.

The wolf was very cross to have been tricked.

"Little pig," he said. "I know where there is a fine tree full of apples."

"Where?" asked the pig.

"At Merrydown," said the wolf, "and if you promise not to trick me, I'll take you there at five o'clock tomorrow morning."

The little pig agreed but next day he got up at four o'clock and went to Merrydown and climbed the apple tree. But it was further away than the turnip field and he was still up the tree when the wolf came loping along.

"What?" said the wolf. "Here before me? Are the apples nice?"

"Very nice," said the pig. "Would you like one?"

He threw an apple quite a long way from the tree and while the wolf was fetching it, the little pig ran down and back to his brick house and shut himself safely indoors.

As soon as he realised he had been tricked again, the wolf raced back to the house of bricks.

"There's a fair," he panted, "this afternoon at Shanklin. I'll come for you at three o'clock if you like."

The pig agreed but at two o'clock he made his own way to the fair. He was having a lovely time eating

toffee apples and candyfloss when he suddenly saw the wolf. Quickly, he climbed into an empty barrel and rolled down the hill towards the wolf.

The wolf was terrified as the barrel rolled faster and

faster. He jumped out of the way and the barrel rolled to the bottom of the hill where the little pig's house was. The pig ran into his house and soon heard the wolf gasping outside.

"Oh dear, what a fright I've had! I went to the fair and a great big round thing rolled down the hill after me and I had to jump out of its way to save my life!"

"Ha!" said the little pig. "That was me inside a barrel!"

The wolf was so angry that he was determined to get the little pig somehow. He started to climb onto the roof. But the little pig guessed what he was up to and put a great big saucepan of water to boil on his fire.

So when the wolf finally managed to squeeze down the chimney, he fell plop into a pan of boiling water! How he howled! The wolf ran out of the little pig's brick house, clutching his burnt bottom . . . and was never seen again.

The Gingerbread Man

Once upon a time a farmer's wife made a batch of gingerbread and with a leftover piece she shaped a little man. You might not think this unusual, because you can see gingerbread men in any baker's window, but this one was the very first such man that had ever been made.

The farmer's wife gave him raisins for eyes and, when he was baked and cooled, she took her icing bag and gave him a bow tie, a mouth and three buttons down his front.

"What a handsome fellow you are!" she exclaimed. "It will be a shame to eat you."

"Eat me!" cried the gingerbread man, sitting up on the baking tray. "No fear—I'm off!"

And he jumped off the table and ran out of the kitchen door. At first the farmer's wife was too astonished to move but, when she saw her sweet treat running away, she set off after him. But he just called out:

"Run, run, fast as you can,

You can't catch me—I'm the Gingerbread Man!"

He had soon put the farm far behind him and found himself in a village. He was running past the butcher's shop when the butcher caught sight of him.

"Stop, let me eat you," cried the butcher.

But the gingerbread man just kept running, calling back over his shoulder:

"Run, run, fast as you can,

You can't catch me—I'm the Gingerbread Man!"

He ran past the blacksmith's and the blacksmith himself came out to look. When he saw the gingerbread man, his mouth watered and he gave chase. But the little man ran on, crying:

"Run, run, fast as you can,

You can't catch me—I'm the Gingerbread Man!"

A little while later he came to the flour mill and the miller ran out to catch him. "Stop, stop!" cried the miller, "I want to eat you up!"

Well, of course, that made the gingerbread man run faster, calling out:

"Run, run, fast as you can,

You can't catch me—I'm the Gingerbread Man!"

By now he was outside the village and running across a field, where he was spotted by a very surprised cow. He nearly ran into her mouth as she munched the grass. She caught a whiff of his delicious smell and started to lumber after him, mooing in such a way that he knew what she intended.

So he ran even faster, crying out to the cow:

"Run, run, fast as you can,

You can't catch me—I'm the Gingerbread Man!"

Now he was in the horse's field and the horse came to

investigate him. "Neigh!" said the horse. "You look tasty. Stop and let me try you."

So the gingerbread man started to sprint, crying:

"Run, run, fast as you can,

You can't catch me—

I'm the Gingerbread Man!"

Suddenly, he realised that he could go no further. There was a stream at the bottom of the field and the horse was behind him. But there was a handsome red fox grooming himself on the bank of the stream and he offered to ferry the gingerbread man across.

The fox was the only being the gingerbread man had met that morning who hadn't wanted to eat him, so he took hold of the fox's tail and the fox started to swim across the stream. Halfway across he said to the gingerbread man, "I am afraid you will get wet. Climb onto my back." So the gingerbread man did.

Three quarters of the way across the stream, the fox said, "I am still afraid you will get wet. Why not climb onto my head?" So the gingerbread man did.

And when they were nearly at the opposite bank, the fox said, "This is the awkward bit. When I get out of the water I have to shake my fur. If you climb onto my nose you will stay dry."

So the gingerbread man climbed onto the fox's nose.

And then the fox flipped up his long red nose, opened his big greedy mouth and swallowed the gingerbread man up in one bite!

And that was the end of the first gingerbread man. Many of them have been made and eaten since and I shouldn't wonder if you've had one yourself.

The Ugly Duckling

It was lovely warm sunny weather when the mother duck laid her eggs in a quiet place by the river. She got very bored with sitting on them, waiting for them to hatch, because she missed her friends in the farmyard.

But at last the eggshells began to crack and the little ducklings poked their heads out. "Oh, what sweet babies!" cried the duck, counting her young. "One, two, three, four, five . . . oh bother! Number six has still not hatched."

The sixth egg was much bigger than all the others and, to tell the truth, the mother duck wasn't sure that it was one of hers. Birds can be very absent-minded about that sort of thing. Still, she sat on it for a few more days and at last it, too, began to crack. And out came the ugliest duckling she had ever seen.

He was much bigger than his pretty little brothers and sisters and had dull grey feathers, while theirs were fluffy yellow and brown.

"Oh dear," thought the mother duck. "Perhaps he's a turkey?"

But the ugly duckling could swim just as well as the others. His mother led them all back down the river to the duck pond in the farmyard.

"Look, here comes another clutch of ducklings," said one of the older ducks. "As if we didn't have enough mouths to feed."

"And look at that one!" said another. "That's the ugliest duckling I've ever seen!" One by one all the ducks in the farmyard noticed the new duckling. And all the hens noticed him. And all the turkeys. And they all said how ugly he was. The poor duckling felt very lonely. The girl who fed the birds was mean to him and tried to kick him. And even his own brothers and sisters teased him and called him names.

So the ugly duckling swam away from the farm along the river and found his own pond. He had no one to talk to, but one day he saw a flock of beautiful white birds flying in the sky. He didn't know what they were but his heart yearned towards them.

"Oh, how lovely to fly free with those beautiful birds," he thought. And he felt very sorry for himself. But he soon felt sorrier, when the warm days of summer were followed by the frosts of autumn and the freezing snow of winter. He had to swim round and round in circles in his pond to stop it from icing over. There was very little to eat and the ugly duckling had a wretched time of it.

Finally the spring came. The flowers started to bloom and fill the air with their scent, and the ugly duckling felt hopeful again. His wings were big and strong now and he started to fly. He flew and flew until he came to a beautiful garden full of flowers with a stream running through it.

The ugly duckling landed in the water and then around the corner came three of the beautiful white birds he had seen the year before.

"I will join them," thought the ugly duckling, "though I'm sure they will jeer at me like all the other birds."

But they didn't. They were three swans and they greeted the ugly duckling like a long-lost brother. He was so shy he lowered his head — and then he saw his own reflection in the water. He wasn't a duck at all — he was a swan!

Some children in the garden saw him and called out, "Look, there's a new swan! And he's much the handsomest."

They threw bread and cake crumbs into the water and made sure the new swan got plenty. The bird who used to be an ugly duckling was so happy. He had gone from being teased and bullied to being the handsomest swan in the garden. He spread his lovely white wings and stretched his lovely white neck and then he hid his head under his wing. He couldn't believe how lucky he was.

Rumpelstiltskin

Once upon a time there was a poor miller who found himself called to do business with a king. You might have thought that would be enough for him, but no, he had to start boasting, so that the king would think he was someone important.

"I have a daughter," he said, which was true enough. "And she is remarkably beautiful," he said, which was also true. But then he added, "And she has this gift, that she can spin straw into gold."

Oh, foolish miller! Why didn't he stop after saying he

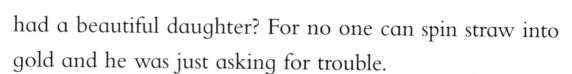

had a beautiful daughter? For no one can spin straw into gold and he was just asking for trouble.

"Really?" said the king, raising his eyebrows and looking at the miller's dusty apron. "That is a very useful gift indeed. Bring her to me so that she may show off this skill."

Now the miller was well and truly in the soup. He wished he had kept his mouth shut, but it was too late for that. He had to bring his daughter to the palace. The king showed her into a large room full of straw, with a spinning-wheel in the middle.

"Here you are, my dear," he said, kindly. "As much straw as you like. Turn it all into gold by morning or you must die."

The poor girl didn't know what to do. She hadn't the faintest idea how to start turning straw into gold, any more than you or I do. So she sat on a bale of straw and wept.

Suddenly a funny little man appeared and asked her what was the matter.

"I have to turn all this straw into gold by morning," sobbed the girl, "or I shall die."

"Well, that's nothing to cry about," said the little man. "I can do that. But what will you give me if I do?"

The miller's daughter said she would give him her necklace and the little man agreed. The girl curled up on the straw and slept peacefully all night to the hum of the spinning-wheel, until the little man needed the bale she was lying on, because he had filled every reel with spun gold.

By dawn the little man had disappeared and the room was full of reels of gold. The king couldn't believe his eyes and the miller's daughter was mightily relieved. But, that evening, the king took her to an even bigger room with even more straw in it and gave her a spinning-wheel.

"You did so well yesterday," he said, smiling. "I'm sure you will manage to turn this lot of straw into gold, too."

The girl wasn't sure at all, until the little man appeared again. He looked at all the straw.

"What will you give me this time?" he asked.

"The ring from my finger," said the girl, taking it off. And, though it was of no great value, the little man took it and set to work. By morning the room was full of spun gold.

And was the king content? You can probably guess by now what he did.

He took the miller's daughter into a barn, filled with straw from floor to ceiling, so that there was scarcely room for the spinning-wheel to be squeezed in.

"This is the last time I shall ask you, my dear," said the king. "But if you turn all this straw into gold, I shall make you my queen." (For the miller's daughter really was very pretty.) "But," added the king, "if you do not, I'm afraid the terms are as before and you will die."

The girl sat at the spinning-wheel and wept. It didn't even cheer her up to see the little man appear, for she knew she had nothing left to give him.

"What, nothing?" he asked, when she explained the situation.

"Nothing at all," she said.

"All right," said the little man. "I will do it for you, but you must promise me that, if you ever become queen, you will give me your first-born child."

So the girl promised; what else could she do? And by morning the whole barn was filled with spun gold. The king clasped her in his arms and kissed her and she was queen within a week.

It had all happened so suddenly that it seemed like a dream and she forgot all about her promise. A year after the marriage, the young queen gave birth to a healthy baby boy. She was delighted with him, like any new mother. But while she was cooing over her pretty baby, the funny little man suddenly appeared in the royal bedroom and reminded her of her promise.

She was horrified. "You can't mean it!" she cried, clutching her

precious baby son. "I shall never give him up. Think of something else."

And she offered him all the riches of her husband's kingdom—jewels, gold, carriages, houses. But the little man tapped his foot impatiently.

"What do I want with all that stuff? You know I can turn even straw into gold. I want something alive."

But when he saw how distressed the queen was, he gave her one more chance.

"I'll give you three days to guess my name. If you can't, then the child is mine." Then he vanished. The next day he was back and the queen began, "Is your name Caspar? Melchior? Balthasar . . . ?" and she worked her way through all the names in the Bible. But, by the end of the day, the little man had said no to every one.

On the second day, she tried all the weird names she could think of, like Shortshanks and Grungefoot and Lumpybottom. The little man became more and more insulted, but the queen still hadn't discovered his real name.

That night she was in despair as she rocked her baby boy. She thought she would never guess the little man's name in time. Then she heard two of her servants talking. One had been out in the forest and had come to a hut with a fire outside it.

"And dancing round the fire was a funny little man singing a song," said the servant. "It went like this:

'Today I'll brew, tomorrow bake,
Then have the princeling, no mistake.
I need no fortune nor no fame,
RUMPELSTILTSKIN is my name!'"

The queen was so excited. Next day, when the little man came, she asked, "Is your name Leonardo?"

"No," said the little man.

"Is your name Brad?"

"No, no," said the little man. "You'll never get it!"

"Then," asked the queen, "is your name . . . Rumpelstiltskin?"

"Who told you, who told you?" screamed the little man, stamping his foot on the floor in such a rage that it went right through the floorboards. He pulled at his leg so hard that he split himself in half, and that was the end of Rumpelstiltskin.